The *Zen*

of Chocolate

Wisdom by the Bar

LAINE CUNNINGHAM

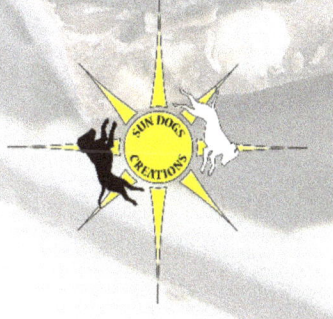

The Zen of Chocolate
Wisdom by the Bar

Published by Sun Dogs Creations
Changing the World One Book at a Time
Softcover ISBN: 9780998224015
Hardcover ISBN: 9781946732002

Cover Design by Angel Leya

Copyright © 2017 and 2019 Laine Cunningham

All rights reserved. No part of this book may be reproduced in any form or by any means, electronic, mechanical, digital, photocopying or recording, except for the inclusion in a review, without permission in writing from the publisher.

Introduction

Chocolate has inspired wonder and delight for millennia. As early at 400 AD, the Maya were drinking chocolate in ceremonies and as a daily refreshment. Europeans were introduced to the beverage in the 16th century.

One missionary, who was less than impressed, noted the drink's unpleasant flavor and the "scum" or froth that topped each cup. With the addition of sugar or honey, however, chocolate became all the rage in Spanish royal courts. Vanilla, pepper and other spices were added to enhance the flavor.

Between the warm spices and the caffeine boost, the drink was long considered healthy. Modern science has backed up those health claims. In addition to the physical benefits, this decadent treasure boosts our minds and bolsters our spirits.

From darkest black to milk white, chocolate and cocoa enhance appetizers, entrees, mixed drinks and desserts. By stimulating the senses of taste, touch and smell, the confection demands that we focus fully on the present. In this meditative moment, the mind expands and *The Zen of Chocolate* delivers wisdom by the bar.

That which is dark can inspire the light.

The richness of chocolate is a wealth that is easily shared.

One delight enrobing another enriches both.

Candy is not always chocolate.
Nor is chocolate always candy.

Pleasure nurtures the body as much as the mind.

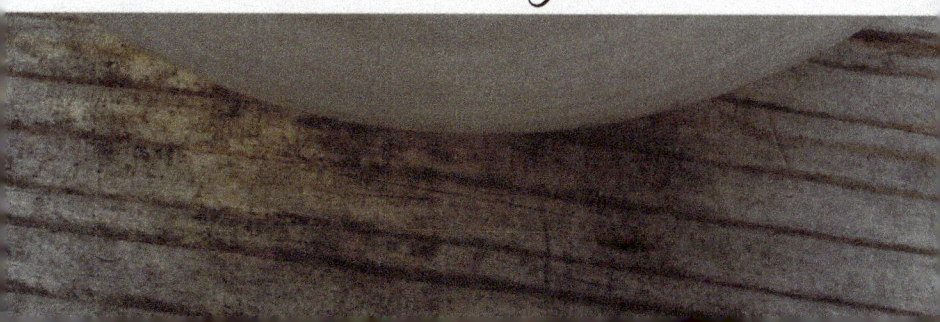

Chocolate that has bloomed retains its rich flavor.

A chocolatier is not a chocolate maker.

Only the ripe pod
produces a useable bean.

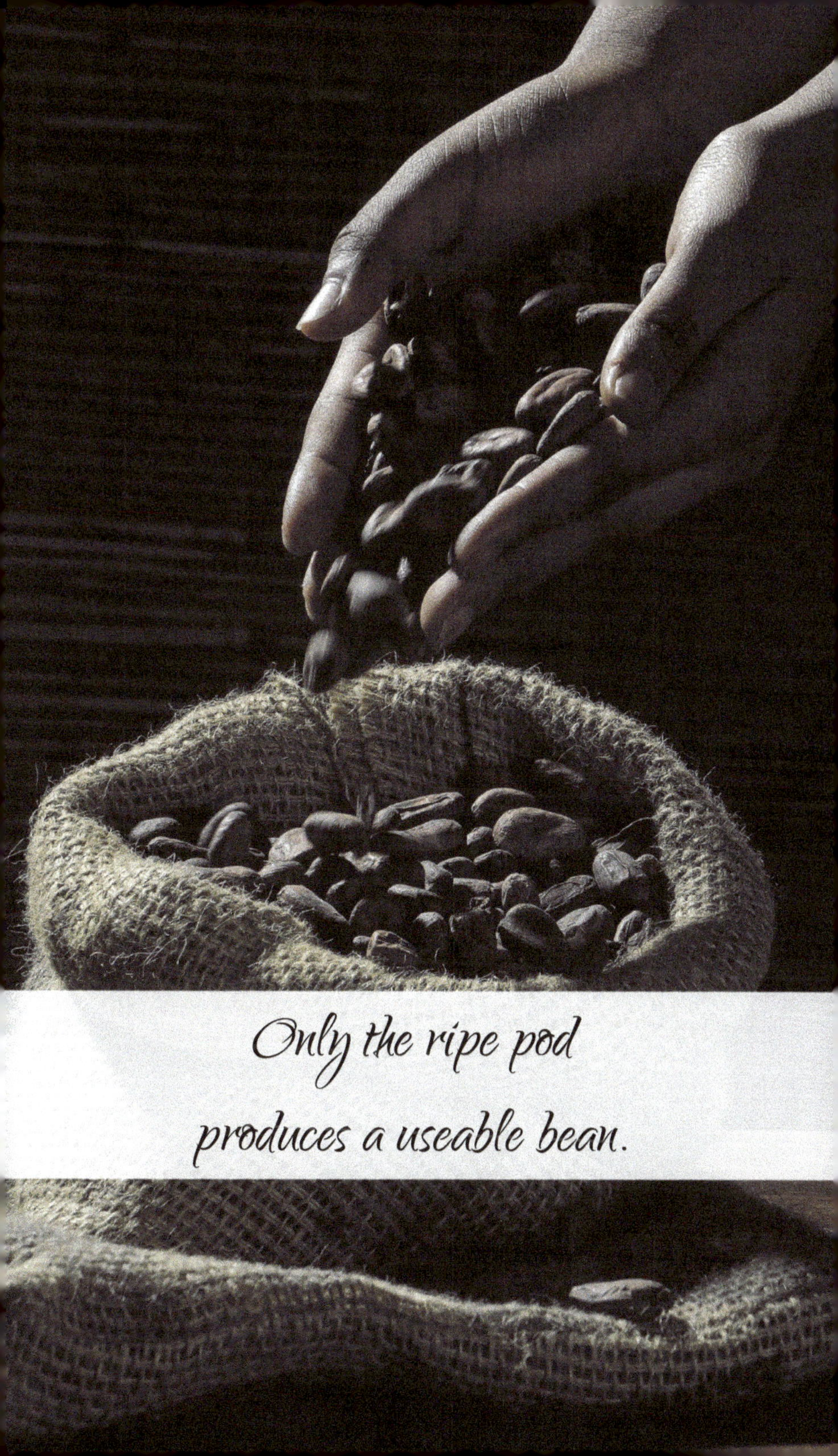

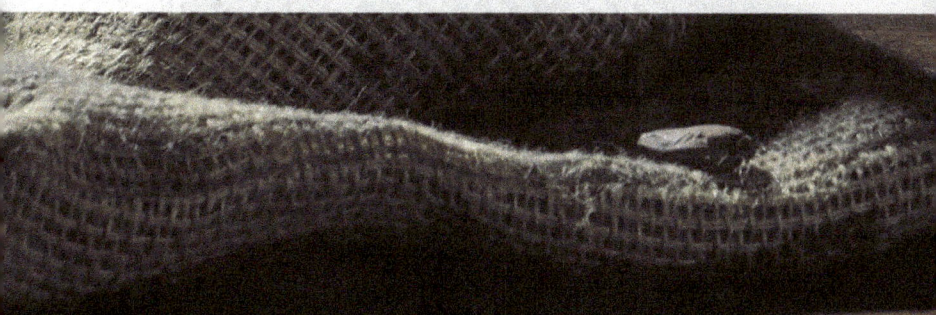

"Chocolate" is a different word for "celebration."

Smoothness comes only after prolonged grinding.

Chocolate is the answer that needs no question.

Moderation is not always a virtue.

Chocolate, like love, is intense and powerful.

One drop of chocolate can sweeten the acerbic tongue.

Multiple textures produce a singular experience.

Excuses are not required for daily celebrations.

Happiness is always within reach.

Chocolate and life are bitter and sweet.

Pleasure spurs guilt only within the meek.

A tiny box can carry great weight.

That which seems simple can be deeply complex.

*Pleasure is a gift
you give to yourself.*

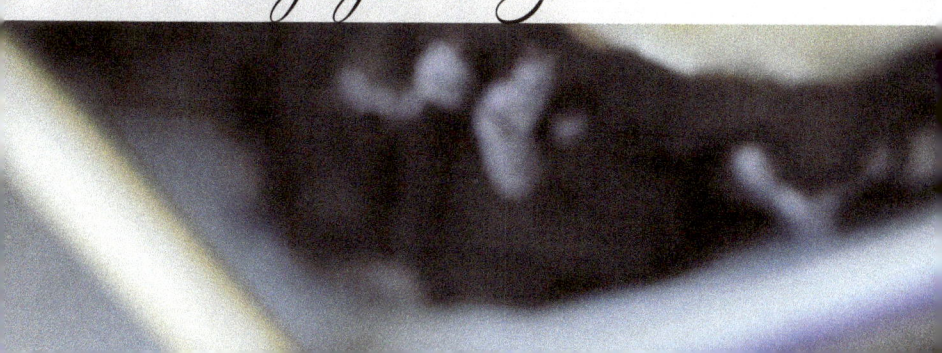

Variety is limited only by the imagination.

The history of chocolate is the history of mankind.

To indulge is human as well as divine.

Complexity offers special rewards.

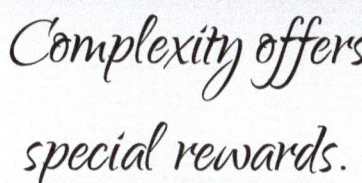

A gilded wrapper does not determine worth.

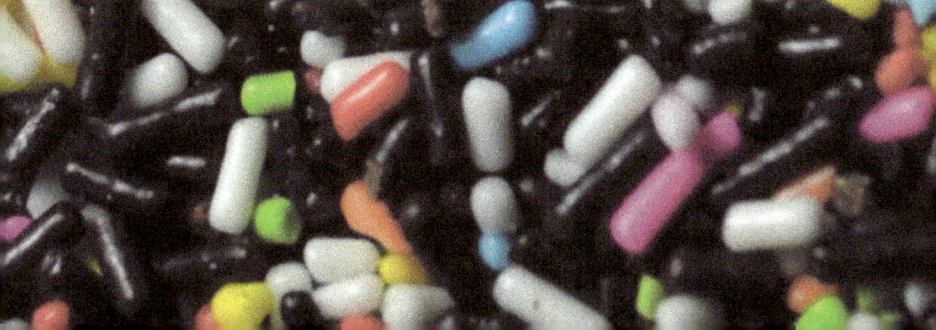

Delight in small things is a foundation for joy.

That which is fleeting

is also priceless.

The senses of the body nourish the elemental soul.

The spice of life is often sweet.

That which is savored soothes the harried mind.

The memory of delight prolongs our joy.

That which is delectable need not be costly.

Certain treasures are universally valued.

Guilt should never cloud your joy.

A delicate nature deserves special care.

The raw pod dispenses only bitterness.

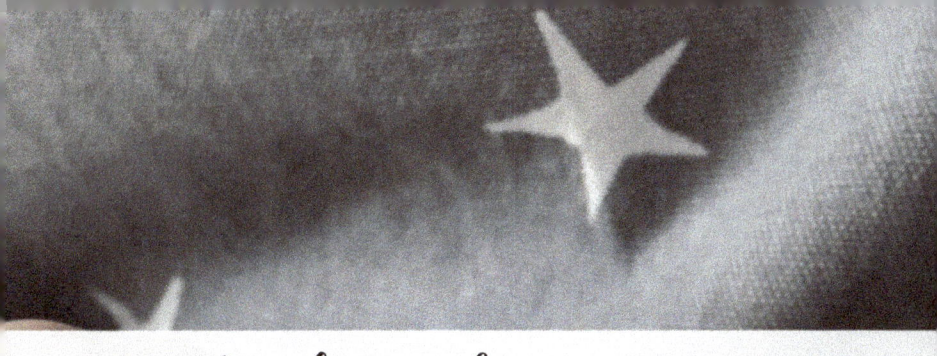

A single cup of cocoa requires plant, animal, and human.

A truffle is a trifle and a treasure.

Sweetness is balanced by that which is bitter.

Wonder is an everyday event.

Hedonism and health can be companions.

Carry sweetness into battle and the war will be won.

About the Author

Laine Cunningham's books take readers on adventures around the world. *The Family Made of Dust* is set in the Australian Outback, while *Reparation* is a novel of the American Great Plains. Her women's travel adventure memoir *Woman Alone: A Six-Month Journey Through the Australian Outback* appeals to fans of *Wild* and *Eat Pray Love*. Her work has received multiple awards including the Hackney and the James Jones Fellowship, and has been published by *Reed*, *Birmingham Arts Journal*, and the annual anthology by *Writer's Digest*. She is the senior editor of *Sunspot Literary Journal*.

Fiction

The Family Made of Dust
Beloved
Reparation

Nonfiction

Woman Alone
On the Wallaby Track: Australian Words and Phrases
Seven Sisters: Messages from Aboriginal Australia
Writing While Female or Black or Gay
The Wisdom of Puppies
The Wisdom of Babies
The Wisdom of Weddings

The Zen of Travel
The Zen of Gardening
Zen in the Stable
The Zen of Chocolate
The Zen of Dogs

Bikes of Berlin
Necropolises of New Orleans I & II
Ruins of Rome I & II
Ancients of Assisi I & II
Panoramas of Portugal
Nuances of New York
Glimpses of Germany
Impressions of Italy
Altitudes of the Alps
Knights Through the Ages
Utopia of the Unicorn
Portraits of Paris
Flourishes of France

www.ingramcontent.com/pod-product-compliance
Lightning Source LLC
Chambersburg PA
CBHW040331300426
44113CB00020B/2720